SINGBOOK

twelve songs worth singing

piano vocal score

YOUTH MUSIC

Foreword

In the coming years Youth Music will be promoting and supporting singing as one of its five main aims. While popular culture features a great deal of singing and singers, too few children get a chance to learn about the life-enhancing thrill of singing together. Our voices are 'built-in' to us and provide us with the most accessible and wonderful musical instrument. Sharing that experience with a group of others enables children to form life-long friendships as well as a life-long love for singing and music.

Following the success of Youth Music's 2002 commission of Tolga Kashif's *Drop in the Ocean*, which reached just under a million children and young people, we decided to commission twelve new, diverse songs that children and young people would really love singing.

Singbook is a new type of singing manual. It is a resource for singing leaders. It provides advice on good singing practice and context for each song to enable meaning and interpretation to meet music making. It provides leads to other songs and themes, and indicates links to the National Curriculum in art, humanities, citizenship, maths, history and sciences.

We hope that people who would like to lead singing for the first time will value the book as well as those who are on the look-out for new ideas.

Youth Music has not worked alone on Singbook. Thanks must go to our Trustees, to the NASUWT, which has provided generous financial support, and Faber Music whose staff have provided advice and counsel concerning the business of publishing. We thank too all the organisations that champion singing in the UK and which have provided advice and encouragement; we consider these organisations our friends and partners.

Christina Coker
Chief Executive Youth Music, April 2005

First published in 2005 by Youth Music and Faber Music Ltd
National Foundation for Youth Music, One America Street, London SE1 0NE
Bloomsbury House, 74–77 Great Russell Street , London WC1B 3DA
Cover design by Greg Jakobek, Warsaw
Cover photo: Digitalvision
Music processed by Jeanne Roberts
Printed in England by Caligraving Ltd

ISBN10: 0-571-52399-4
EAN13: 978-0-571-52399-3

To buy Singbook, please contact your local music retailer or Faber Music sales enquiries:
Faber Music Ltd, Burnt Mill, Elizabeth Way, Harlow, CM20 2HX England

Tel: +44 (0) 1279 82 89 82 Fax: +44 (0) 1279 82 89 83
sales@fabermusic.com fabermusic.com

Contents

Refuge

music & lyrics by
Howard Goodall

14
they leave be-hind? What sights, what sounds, what thoughts are on their mind?
have you sur-vived? What hopes, what dreams were left when you ar-rived?
1.
2. I've
Gmaj7 F#m7/A Bm Bm7/A E9/G#
1.
18
2.
C
with confidence
ALL
f
Who'll be your re-fuge, your shel-ter, your for-tress? Who'll be your cham-pion?
2.
G D D/C# Bm Em7
f
22
Who'll be your re-fuge, your pi-lot, your bro-ther, your north-ern star?
G D D/C# Bm G/B F#m
26
D
Who will be your se-cond sight; the light that guides your way at night? Don't be down-heart-ed.
F#m7 Am G Em

30
I'll be your re - fuge, I'll be your re - fuge.
G D Bm7/D G/D D
34
Parts 1 & 2
E
mf with feeling
3. There's no - thing wrong with be - ing shy and ev - 'ry - bo - dy knows that fools speak
Parts 3 & 4
Bm7/D D/A G/B
mf
37
with purpose
loud - er than the rest. Let no - one tell you how to think or what is right or true: you are not
mf
(3.) that fools speak loud - er than the rest.
G Em D/A G/B
41
F
reflectively
weak or se - cond best. What crimes, what hurt, what wars
reflectively
you are not weak or se - cond best. What crimes, what hurt,
G Em Bm Bm7/A

45
Part 1
building in strength and determination
have you sur - vived?
What hopes,
what dreams
Part 2
building in strength and determination
have you sur - vived?
What hopes,
what dreams
Part 3
what wars have you sur - vived?
building in strength and determination
What hopes,
Part 4
what wars have you sur - vived?
building in strength and determination
What hopes,
Gmaj7
F♯m/A
Bm
48
were left when you ar - rived?
were left when you ar - rived?
what dreams
were left when you ar - rived?
what dreams
were left when you ar - rived?
G
f strong and proud
I'll be your
Bm/A
E9/G♯
G
f
52
(ALL)
re - fuge, your shel - ter, your for - tress, I'll be your cham - pion.
I'll be your
D
D/C♯
Bm7
Em7
G

56
H
re - fuge, your pi - lot, your bro - ther, your north - ern star.
I will be your se - cond sight; the
D D/C♯ Bm7 G/B F♯m F♯m F♯m7
60
Parts 1 & 2
light that guides your way at night. Don't be down - heart - ed.
I
I'll be your
Parts 3 & 4
(2nd time only)
(re - fuge,)
Am G Em G
64
re - fuge, I'll be your re - fuge,
I'll be your re - fuge, I'll be your
D Bm7/D G/D D
67
I'll be your re - fuge.
re - fuge, re - fuge.
Bm7/D G/D D D (no 3rd)
ff

Ame sau vala tara bal

(*We are all your children*)

music & lyrics by
Nirmala Shah

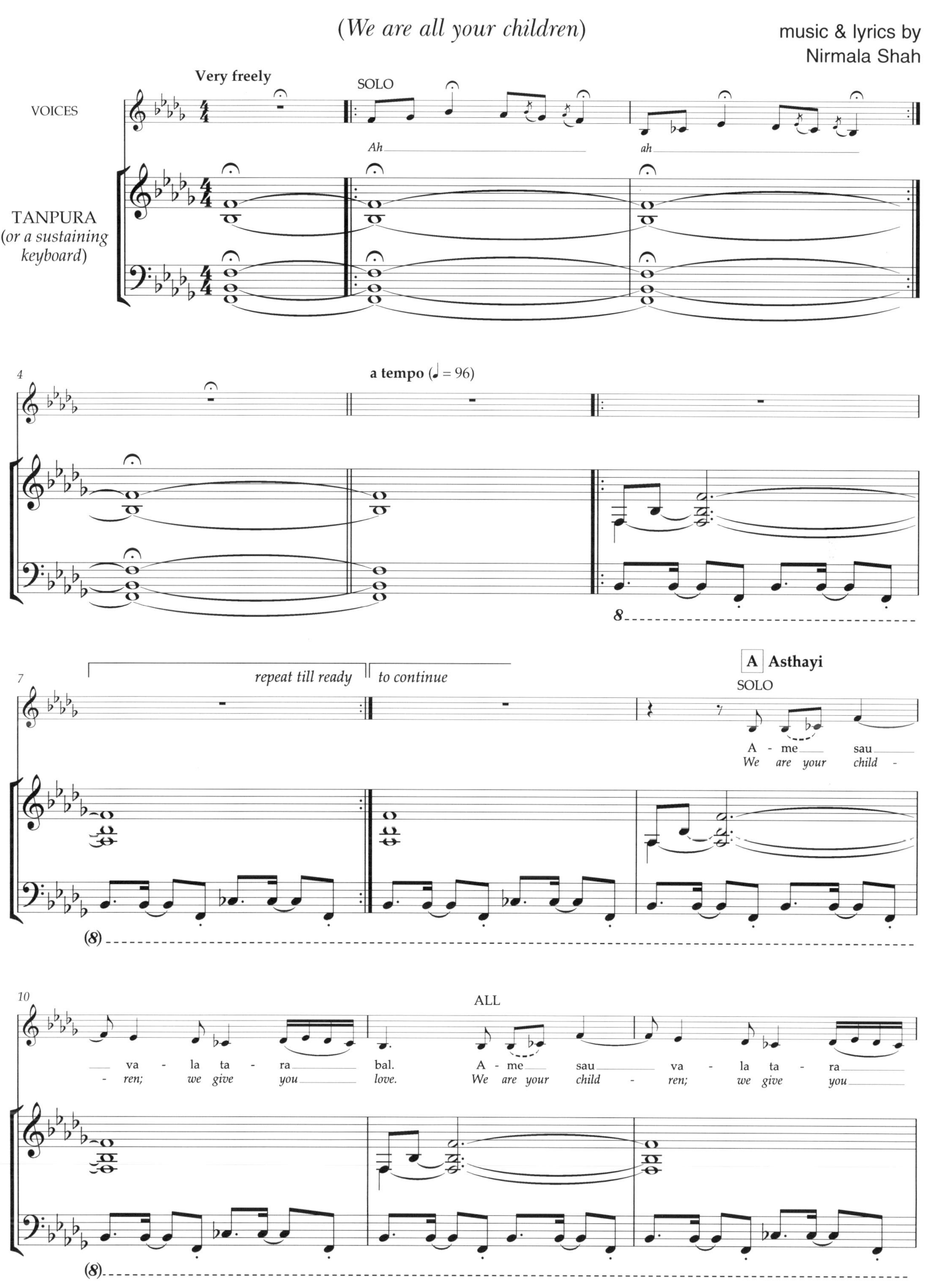

13
SOLO
bal. A - me sau va - la ta - ra bal.
love. We are your child - ren; we give you love.
ALL
A - me sau
We are your child -
(8ve basso sempre)
16
va - la ta - ra bal.
- ren; we give you love.
SOLO
A - me sau va - la ta - ra
We are your child - ren; we give you
19
ALL
bal. A - me sau va - la ta - ra bal.
love. We are your child - ren; we give you love.
B 1st Antara
23
SOLO
Sa - tya bo - la - vu ne sa - tya su - na - vu.
Let the Truth be spo - ken; And let the Truth be heard.

27
ALL
SOLO
Sa - tya bo - la - vu ne sa - tya su - na - vu. Ay - vi a - ma - ri
Let the Truth be spo - ken; And let the Truth be heard. That is the way we should
(8)
30
ALL
Asthayi
tek. Ay - vi a - ma - ri tek. A - me sau
live. That is the way we should live. We are your child -
33
va - la ta - ra bal. A - me sau va - la ta - ra
- ren; we give you love. We are your child - ren; we give you
8
36
bal. A - me sau va - la ta - ra bal.
love. We are your child - ren; we give you love.
(8ve basso sempre)

39
C 2nd Antara
SOLO
Pre - ma - nu man - di - ra ne
And may we show com - pas sion
43
ALL
pre - ma - ni pra - ti - ma.
for ev - 'ry liv - ing be - ing.
Pre - ma - nu man - di - ra ne
And may we show com - pas - sion
pre - ma - ni pra - ti - ma.
for ev - 'ry liv - ing be - ing.
46
SOLO
ALL
Pu - ja a - ma - ri nek.
These are the gifts we bring.
Pu - ja a - ma - ri
These are the gifts we
49
Asthayi
nek. A - me sau va - la ta - ra bal. A - me sau
bring. We are your child - ren; we give you love. We are your child -
8

52
va - la ta - ra bal. A - me sau va - la ta - ra
- ren; we give you love. We are your child - ren; we give you
(8ve basso sempre)
55
bal.
love.
D 3rd Antara
59
SOLO
ALL
Da - ya ra - khi ye sau pra - ni pa - ra. Da - ya ra - khi ye
And so we of - fer love, we of - fer love and mer - cy. And so we of - fer love,
62
SOLO
sau pra - ni pa - ra. A - vo a - ma - ro vi - vek.
we of - fer love and mer - cy. That is the way it should be.

E Asthayi
ALL
A - vo a - ma - ro vi - vek. A - me sau va - la ta - ra bal. A - me sau va - la ta - ra bal. A - me sau va - la ta - ra
That is the way it should be. We are your child - ren; we give you love. We are your child - ren; we give you love. We are your child - ren; we give you
bal, va - la ta - ra bal, va - la ta - ra bal, va - la ta - ra bal, va - la ta - ra bal.
love, we will give you love, we will give you love, we will give you love, we will give you love.
8
SA RE GA MA PA DHA NI SA SA NI DHA PA MA GA RE SA
Kaherwa Taal (8 beats):
dha ghe na ti na ka dhin na
Tabla pattern in the song:
Hi-hat or finger cymbal:
Bells or small clashing cymbals:

The smile behind the eyes

music & lyrics by
Brenda Rattray

9
bird can fly. I'm sail - ing in the sky.
o - ver moun - tains. I am soar - ing high.
love and peace;
Dn dn dn dn dn dn dn dn dn, dn dn dn dn dn dn dn dn dn.
A♭
Cm/E♭
B♭m/E♭
Cm/E♭ B♭m/E♭
13
Sail, I'm sail - ing fur - ther than the sea's ex - panse as I ful - fil my
Watch me in your dreams; I'll vi - sit you some - time and tell you of my
Kind - - ness, res - - - - pect;
Dn dn dn dn dn dn dn dn dn, dn dn dn dn dn dn dn dn dn.
A♭
B♭m7/A♭
A♭
B♭m7/A♭
17
jour - ney; join the an - gels in the sky.
jour - ney. For I'm in a - no - ther time.
1.
we all need.
Dn dn dn dn dn dn dn dn dn, dn dn dn dn dn.
A♭
E♭
A♭
1.

C CHORUS
2.
Don't you wor - ry, don't you cry. I am soar-
Don't you wor - ry, don't you cry. I am soar-
Dn dn dn dn dn dn dn dn dn, dn dn dn dn dn dn dn dn dn.
2.
E♭ D♭ A♭
- ing, fly - ing high. You will find
- ing, fly - ing high. You will find
Dn dn dn dn dn dn dn dn dn, dn dn dn dn dn dn dn dn dn.
E♭ D♭ A♭
me, in the smile behind the eyes of those peo-
me, in the smile behind the eyes of those peo-
Dn dn dn dn dn dn dn dn dn, dn dn dn dn dn dn dn dn dn.
E♭ D♭ A♭

34
1.
- ple who just dai - ly pass you by.
Don't you wor -
- ple who just dai - ly pass you by.
Don't you wor -
Dn dn dn dn dn dn dn dn dn, dn dn dn dn dn dn dn dn dn.
1.
E♭
D♭
38
2.
- ple who just dai - ly pass you by.
- ple who just dai - ly pass you by.
Dn dn dn dn dn dn dn dn dn, dn dn dn dn dn.
2.
E♭7
A♭
42
repeat till ready
mf
Dn dn dn dn dn dn dn dn dn, dn dn dn dn dn.
A♭
B♭m7/A♭
repeat till ready
A♭
mf

D
46
mf
3. If you have a mo - ment when you think of me, and sud - den - ly a
4. Serve your neigh-bour, love your e - ne - my; He's here to teach you pa - tience,
mf 2nd time only
(4.) Sing a song of
mp
Dn dn dn dn dn dn dn dn dn, dn dn dn dn dn dn dn dn dn.
A♭ B♭m7/A♭ A♭ B♭m7/A♭
50
sad - ness hits you, and you start to cry.
love, res - pect; the ba - sics we all need.
love and peace;
Dn dn dn dn dn dn dn dn dn, dn dn dn dn dn dn dn dn dn.
A♭ Cm/E♭ B♭m/E♭ Cm/E♭ B♭m/E♭
54
Just re - mem - ber I am fly - ing free, I'm hap - py, for in life I
Sho - wer all of those who hurt you with some love. With - in their hearts there's
Kind - ness, res - pect;
Dn dn dn dn dn dn dn dn dn, dn dn dn dn dn dn dn dn dn
A♭ B♭m7/A♭ A♭ B♭m7/A♭

58
1st verse
2nd verse
did my best, ser - vice to man - kind.
lots of room to plant some lov - ing seeds.
1.
we all need.
Dn dn dn dn dn dn dn dn dn, dn dn dn dn dn.
A♭
E♭
A♭
1.
E BRIDGE
62
2.
mp
oo - ee oo - ay oo - ee oo - ay, oo - ee oo - ay oo - ee
Here's a lov - ing seed for you, here's a lov - ing seed for you, here's a lov - ing
Fm/C Cm E♭/C Cm Fm/C Cm E♭/C
68
oo - ay, oo - ee oo - ay, oo - ee oo - ay, oo - ee,
seed for you, here's a lov - ing seed for you, here's a lov - ing seed for you, here's a lov - ing
Cm Fm/C Cm E♭/C Cm Fm/C Cm E♭/C

74
oo - ay, oo - ee oo - ay.
seed for you, here's a lov - ing seed for you, here's a lov - ing seed for you, here's a lov - ing
oo - ay, oo - ee oo - ay.
Cm
D♭
E♭
80
F
mf
Sing a song for me
seed for you, here's a lov - ing seed for you, here's a lov - ing seed for you.
A♭
mf
86
some - time, help some - one; bless a strang - er.
mf
Sing a song for me some - time; bless a strang - er as he pas - ses by,
mp
a song for me some - time, a song for me some - time, re - mem - ber me,
E♭
A♭
E♭7
A♭

91
Ev - 'ry good deed, thought and kind word said,
as he pas - ses by.
re-mem - ber me.
a song for me
E♭
E♭7
A♭
E♭
95
wings you'll wear,
join me in the sky.
Ev - 'ry good deed, thought and kind words said,
join me in the sky.
some-time,
a song for me
some-time,
join me in the sky.
A♭
E♭7
A♭
E♭7
A♭
100
f
oo-ee oo - ay oo - ee oo - ay,
oo-ee oo -
f
Here's a lov - ing seed for you,
here's a lov - ing seed for you,
f
oo-ee oo - ay oo - ee oo - ay,
oo-ee oo -
Fm/C
Cm
E♭/C
Cm
Fm/C
f

105
-ay oo - ee oo - ay, oo - ee oo - ay, oo - ee oo - ay,
here's a lov - ing seed for you, here's a lov - ing seed for you, here's a lov - ing seed for you,
-ay oo - ee oo - ay, oo - ee oo - ay, oo - ee oo - ay,
Cm E♭/C Cm Fm/C Cm E♭/C Cm Fm/C
111
oo - ee, oo - ay, oo - ee oo - ay.
here's a lov - ing seed for you, here's a lov - ing seed for you, here's a lov - ing
oo - ee, oo - ay, oo - ee oo - ay.
Cm E♭/C Cm D♭ E♭
116
repeat and fade to nothing
seed for you, here's a lov - ing seed for you, here's a lov - ing seed for you.

Believe

music & lyrics by
Lin Marsh

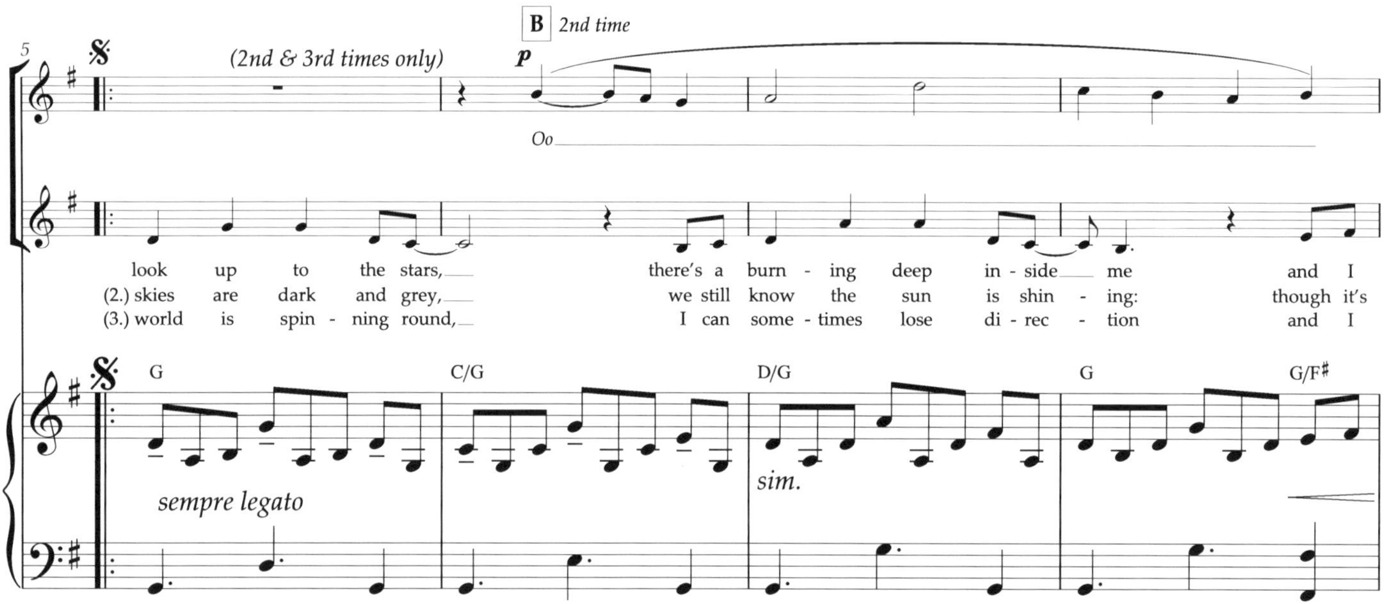

oo
some - thing I can sense, deep with - in a dream to guide me, and I
long as I be - lieve, there is no - thing I can't wish for; not a
friends a - round to care, there is no - thing I can't han - dle, and I'll
G C/G D/F♯ G G/F♯
mp
cresc.
know that I am reach - ing for my goal.
dream that I'm un - a - ble to ful - fill.
face the fu - ture trea - sur - ing each day.
C
with conviction
last time: with strength
f
I can do a -
Em Cmaj7 D7sus4 D
D 2nd time
mf
Ah
ah
- ny - thing at all, I can climb the high - est moun - tain, I can feel the o - cean
G C D/F♯ G/B G/F♯ Em7

cresc.
ah
calling wild and free.
I can be anything I want, with this
Cmaj7
D7sus4
D
G
C
3rd time to Coda
dim.
if I can just believe in me.
hope to drive me onward, if I can just believe in me.
B7/D#
Em
Em/D
C
C/D
G
1.
2.
E
Bridge/Middle Eight
mf with confidence
I'll find it somehow.
mp
2. When the
And whatever it takes I'll find it somehow; what-
E♭
B♭/D
mf

40
I'll show I'm strong, I'll show I'm strong. I'll make it hap - pen:
ev - er it needs I'll show I'm strong. What - ev - er it takes I'll make it hap - pen:
E♭
B♭/D
A♭
E♭/G
Go to 𝄋 and then to Coda 𝄌
F
44
find - ing out where I be - long.
mf
find - ing out where I be - long.
3. While the
Go to 𝄋 and then to Coda 𝄌
Am7/D
D7
Am7/D
D7sus4
D7
CODA
rit.
48
cresc. sempre
ff
just be - lieve in me.
cresc. sempre
ff
just be - lieve in me.
CODA
C
C/D
G
rit.
C6/G
G
cresc. sempre
ff

Building

music & lyrics by
Richard Stilgoe

D
34
Part 2
p
Put your trea - sures a - way in a safe place. Put your
E♭ A♭ E♭ A♭ E♭ B♭7
39
trea - sures a - way in a safe place. So build your - self a safe place to -
E♭ E♭7 A♭ B♭7 E♭ D♭
45
Part 1
mp
We put
Part 2
p sub.
- day, and put your - self a - way.
C7 C7/E F9 B♭7 E♭ A♭ A♭/B♭ E♭ A♭ E♭ B♭7
p sub.
51
some - thing where no - thing was be - fore. We build win - dows
mp
Put your trea - sures a - way in a safe place. Put your
E♭ A♭ E♭ A♭ E♭ B♭7

56
and o - pen the door.
We bring the out - side in - side, turn no - thing in - to
trea - sures a - way in a safe place. So build your - self a safe place to -
E♭ E♭7 A♭ B♭7 E♭ D♭
62
Part 1
p sub.
more. We put some - thing where no - thing was be - fore.
E
Part 2
p sub.
- day, and put your - self a - way.
Part 3
mf
It's just
C7 C7/E F9 B♭7 E♭ A♭ A♭/B♭ E♭ A♭ E♭ B♭7
sub. p
68
(Part 3)
one thing on top of a - no - ther, and a - no - ther and a - no - ther and a - no - ther! It's just one thing on
E♭ E♭/G Cm7/A♭ A♭ E♭ A♭ E♭ B♭7 Fm7
mf
73
top of a - no - ther, and a - no - ther and a - no - ther and a - no - ther! Ev - 'ry brick sits on its fa - ther and mo - ther and it's
B♭7 E♭ A♭/B♭ E♭ E♭/B♭ A♭ B♭ B♭7

78
squeezed be-tween its sis - ter and its bro - ther, It's just one thing on top of a - no - ther, and a -
E♭ B♭m/D♭ C7 C7/G F B♭7 E♭ E♭/G A♭maj9 A♭6
F
83
Part 1
mp
We put some - thing where no - thing was be -
Part 2
mp (2. mf)
Put your trea - sures a -
Part 3
mp
- no - ther and a - no - ther and a - no - ther! It's just one thing on top of a - no - ther, and a -
E♭ A♭ E♭ B♭7 E♭ A♭maj9 A♭
mp
2nd time unaccompanied
87
- fore. We build win - dows and o - pen the door.
-way in a safe place. Put your trea - sures a -
- no - ther and a - no - ther and a - no - ther! It's just one thing on top of a - no - ther, and a -
E♭ A♭ E♭ B♭7 B♭/F B♭7

91
We bring the out - side in - side, turn
way in a safe place. So build your - self a
- no - ther and a - no - ther and a - no - ther! Ev - 'ry brick sits on its fa - ther and mo - ther and it's
E♭ E♭/B♭ E♭ E♭/B♭ A♭ B♭9
95
no - thing in - to more.
We put some - thing where
safe place to - day,
and put your - self a -
squeezed be - tween its sis - ter and its bro - ther, It's just one thing on
E♭ B♭m/D♭ C C7/G F7 B♭7 E♭ Cm/E♭
mp
G
99
no - thing was be - fore.
We put We put
- way.
top of a - no - ther, and a - no - ther and a - no - ther and a - no - ther! It's just - no - ther! It's just
1. 2.
mf f
A♭maj9 A♭6 E♭ A♭ E♭ N.C. D7

103
some - thing where no-thing was be - fore. We build
f
Put your trea - sures a - way in a safe place.
one thing on top of a - no - ther, and a - no-ther and a - no-ther and a - no-ther! It's just
G Cmaj9 C G C G
107
win - dows and o-pen the door. We
Put your trea - sures a - way in a safe place. So
one thing on top of a - no - ther, and a - no-ther and a - no-ther and a - no-ther! Ev-'ry
D D/A D7 G G/D G G/D
111
bring the out-side in - side, turn no - thing in - to more. We put
f
build your - self a safe place to - day, and
f
brick sits on its fa-ther and mo - ther and it's squeezed be-tween its sis - ter and its bro - ther, It's just
C D9 G Dm/F E E7/B A7 D7

116
H
ff
some - thing where nothing was before.
We put some-thing where
put your - self a - way.
We put some-thing where
one thing on top of a - no - ther, and a - no ther and a - no - ther and a - no - ther!
We put some-thing where
G Em/G Cma7 C6 G C G D7 G
121
I
no - thing was.
Prove that we were here, be - cause there's some - thing where
C G F E7 E7/G♯ A9
drum fill
126
no - thing was be - fore.
C G/B B° Am7 G C G C G
* G optional

Hey, Escher!

'... it's another world', as my Mother used to say

music & lyrics by
Barry Russell

𝄋

A I

♩ = 96

1. *repeat till ready* 2. ALL ***f*** *conversational*

Hey, Es - cher! Is it day or night? It's

C/D Bb/G Bb/G C/D Bb/G

f *sim.*

6

hard to make it out from where I'm stand - ing! No

C/D Bb/G C/D Bb/G C/D Bb/G

12

pres - sure. Is it black or white? Where am I? The ho - ri - zon's ne - ver end - ing!

C/D Bb/G C/D Bb/G C/D Bb/G

18

B J

mf *with wonder*

1. Once in - side your pic - ture frame, play - ing at your mind game,

Bb/D C/D D Em/D F/D Gm7 C Gm7 C

3 3 3

mf

24
cresc. poco a poco
find - ing no - thing's quite the same as the world out - side. Ed - ges blur and in - ter - sect,
Gm7 C Am7 D Dm7 Gm7 C
cresc. poco a poco
30
increasingly confident
where do all the lines con - nect? Pat - terns grow and shapes re - flect, and I'd like to come ex - plore
Gm7 C Gm7 C Am7 D Dm7 Bm/D Am/D
36
to Coda
C
f
in - side. Hey,
G/D E♭/D E♭/C Am C/D B♭/G C/D B♭/G
f
42
conversational
Es - cher! Is it day or night? It's hard to make it out from where I'm stand - ing!
C/D B♭/G C/D B♭/G C/D B♭/G
sim.
48
No pres - sure. Is it black or white? Where am I? The ho - ri -
C/D B♭/G C/D B♭/G C/D

D
mf
-zon's never ending!
2. Here's a
B♭/G C/D B♭/G C/D D/C E♭/B♭ F
with a sense of discovery
building with a water-fall, a stream that flows up-hill. Hood-ed figures trudg-ing
Cm7 E♭/F F/B♭ Cm7
on-wards but they're real-ly stand-ing still. Stairs shoot off in all di-rec-tions, no-thing's
cresc.
E♭/F F/B♭ Am7 C/D
excited
f
ev-er what it seems. Hey, Es-cher! Night-mare vi-sions, snap-shots ta-ken from my
Gma7 Csus/D Fsus/D♭ A♭/C B♭
E
wild-est dreams.
Hey,
Gsus/A♭ C/D B♭/G C/D B♭/G
sim.

79 conversational
Es - cher! Is it day or night? It's hard to make it out from where I'm stand - ing!
C/D B♭/G C/D B♭/G C/D B♭/G
85
No pres - sure. Is it black or white? Where am I? The ho - ri -
C/D B♭/G C/D B♭/G C/D
90
- zon's ne - ver end - ing!
B♭/G C/D B♭/G B♭/D C/D D Em/D F/D
cresc.
F
95 f with wonder
3. Birds are fish and fish are birds, ci - ties turn - ing in - to words, i - ma - ges that strike a chord
Gm7 C Gm7 C Gm7
100
but they're not quite right. Spin - ning lengths of o - range peel,
C Am7 D Dm7 Gm7 C
p

bold and confident
cresc.
see the fa - ces they re - veal,
ev - 'ry - thing is quite sur - real.
Still I'd like to come
Gm7 C Gm7 C Am7 D Dm7
cresc.
G
SOLO or small group (rock-gospel style or improvise)
It's a -
f with awe and delight
ex - plore in - side ... It's a - no - ther world.
Bm/D Am/D G/D E♭/D F/A E♭/A D F♯m7 D7/F♯
-no-ther world, a - no - ther world.
So take my hand and
ALL
It's a - no - ther world,
F/G G/C Em/A D F♯m7 D7/F♯ F/G
come in - side, wo - o,
it's a - no-ther world take a look in - side,
it's a - no - ther world,
it's a -
G/C Em/A D F♯m7 D7/F♯ F/G G/C Em/A

125
H
it's a - no-ther world, wo - o.
-no - ther world.
mf with a sense of discovery
4. In a cir - cle, si - mi - an
D F♯m7 D7/F♯ F/G F F/B♭ E♭/C
mf
130
crea - tures turn - ing in - to dan - cing men. And then right be - fore your eyes they're chang - ing
E♭/F F/B♭ E♭/C E♭/F
135
cresc.
back to apes a - gain. Mon - sters climb - ing out of pic - tures crawl a - round and melt back
F/B♭ Am7 Am7/D Gma7
cresc.
140
f questioning and bold
in. Hey, Es - cher! Tell me some - thing: where does my world end and yours be - gin?
Csus/D Fsus/D♭ A♭/C B♭ Gsus/A♭
f

Go back to 𝄋
145
C/D
B♭/G
C/D
sim.
CODA
149
f
It's a - no - ther world,
F/A E♭/A D F♯m7 D7/F♯ F/G G/C Em/A
K
with awe and delight
it's a -
154
(repeat and improvise ad lib.)
- no - ther world,
it's a -
D F♯m7 D7/F♯ F/G G/C Em/A
OPTIONAL CHANT/ROUND
Percussion suggestion: CLAVES or SHAKERS
Birds be - come fish ... be - come birds be - come fish ... be - come
Percussion suggestion: SNARE DRUM
... hand draws a hand, draws a hand ... draws it - self! A
Percussion suggestion: BONGOS or AGOGO
... climb - ing out of pic - tures, stroll - ing round and melt - ing back. Crea - tures
Percussion suggestion: DJEMBE
I can't tell
... dark from light or right from left or black from white or day from night.
158
- no - ther world.
D F♯m7 D7/F♯ F/G F/A F/G F/E♭ D

Vera

(Summer)

poem by
Ndre Mjeda (1866–1937)

music by
Akil Koci

12
B
die - lli i dogj. Veç në at ar por si i tre - tun zi ndër pet - ka,
har - vest - ing. Their fa - ces black - en but the reap - ers on - ly toil un - til their
F/G C/F F Gm7 F/G F Gm7
16
ter ndër f'tyrë, po korr nji cu - cë sho - qe t've - tun. Me hi t'vetë që
la - bours end, But one young girl works a - lone and lone - ly, on - ly her sha - dow
F Gm7 F/G C7/G F/G
20
C
mbra - pa merr tash t'tje - ra ve - ra vet e tre - ta korrsh moj bijë me
for a friend. The sum - mers pass and the same girl, old - er, smil - ing where her
C/G F C/F F Gm F/G C/G

24
mo - tra shend. Si vjet unë ve - tun tue kor - të gje - ta pa nji mo - tër
tears once were, A lit - tle sis - ter at each shoul - der, no more lone - li -
mo - tra shend. Si vjet unë ve - tun tue kor - të gje - ta pa nji mo - tër
tears once were, A lit - tle sis - ter at each shoul - der, no more lone - li -
F C/F F Gm F/G C/G
28
pa gaz - mend.
- ness for her.
pa gaz - mend.
- ness for her.
F/G C/F F
D
32
Asht zver - dhun fu - sha e ndër gru - no - re po vlojn' kor - cat
The fields of grain to gold are turn - ing, like the birds the
Asht zver - dhun fu - sha e ndër gru - no - re po vlojn' kor - cat
The fields of grain to gold are turn - ing, like the birds the
C/F F Gm F/G C/G

36
por – si – zogj, kën - dojn' ka - tun - da - rët me mal - so - rë pa kuj - tu se
farm - ers sing, Come high, come low, tho' the sun is burn - ing, hur - ry with your
por - si - zogj, kën - dojn' ka - tun - da - rët me mal - so - rë pa kuj - tu se
farm - ers sing, Come high, come low, tho' the sun is burn - ing, hur - ry with your
F C/F F Gm F/G C/G
40
E
die - lli i dogj. Veç në at ar - por - si i tre - tun zi ndër pet - ka,
har - vest - ing. Their fa - ces black - en but the reap - ers on - ly toil un - til their
die - lli i dogj. Veç në at ar - por - si i tre - tun zi ndër pet - ka,
har - vest - ing. Their fa - ces black - en but the reap - ers on - ly toil un - til their
F/G C/F F Gm7 F/G F Gm7
44
ter ndër f'tyrë, po korr nji cu - cë sho - qe t've - tun. Me hi t'vetë që
la - bours end, But one young girl works a - lone and lone - ly, On - ly her sha - dow
ter ndër f'tyrë, po korr nji cu - cë sho - qe t've - tun. Me hi t'vetë që
la - bours end, But one young girl works a - lone and lone - ly, On - ly her sha - dow
F Gm7 F/G C7/G F/G

F
48
mbra - pa merr tash t'tje - ra ve - ra vet e tre - ta
for a friend. The sum - mers pass and the same girl, old - er,
C/G F C/F F
51
korrsh moj bijë me mo - tra shend. Si vjet unë ve - tun tue
smil - ing where her tears once were, A lit - tle sis - ter
Gm F/G C/G F C/F
54
kor të gje - ta pa nji mo - tër pa gaz - mend.
at each shoul - der, no more lone - li - ness for her.
F Gm F/G C/G F/G C/F F

OK

music & lyrics by
Tyndale Thomas

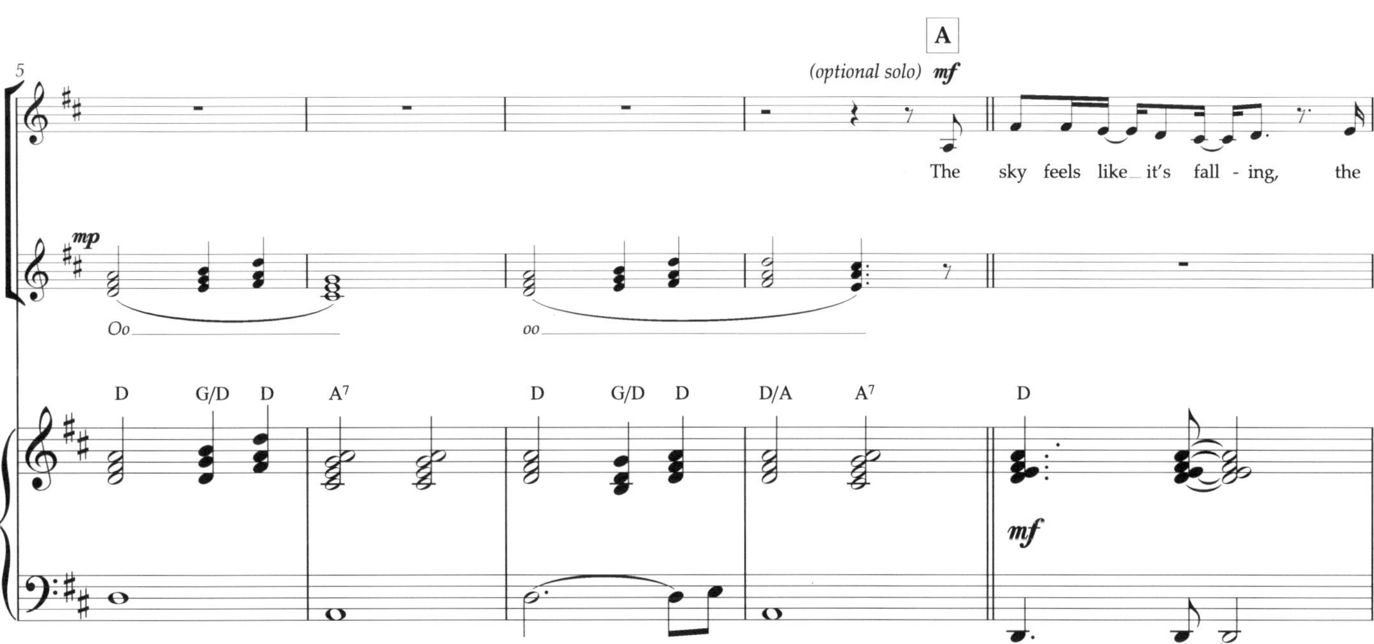

13
world on your shoul - ders and it's bound to pull you down. It's so much clear - er when you
D A7sus4/E D/F♯ A7sus4 D A7sus4/E
B
16
ALL f
reach for high - er ground. Gon - na be all right; gon - na be O K. If you're
A7sus4/F♯ A7sus4 Dsus4/A D D/F♯ D+/F♯
f
19
reach - ing for the light, you're sure to find the way. Gon - na be all right; gon - na be O K.
G Bm7 Em7 A7sus4 D
C
22
Lead vocal
If you're reach - ing for the light, you're sure to find the way.
Backing vocals
f
If you're reach - ing for the light, you're sure to find the way.
D/F♯ D+/F♯ B♭maj7 Am Gm7 A7sus4 D

E
(optional solo) mf
The
mf
Oo
oo
Bm/E A7/F♯ Bm7/G Bm7/A D G/D D A7 D G/D D D/A A7
mf
(Lead vocal)
world keeps on turn - ing, yes - ter - day has gone. Look to the fu - ture, it's a
D A7sus4 D
place where you be - long. Like a flo - wer grow - ing, search - ing for the sun, You can
A7sus4 D A7sus4/E D/F♯ A7sus4
F
ALL f
live: your dreams have on - ly just be - gun. Gon - na be all right;
D A7sus4/E A7sus4/F♯ A7sus4 Dsus4/A
f

38
gon-na be O K.
If you're reach-ing for the light, you're
D
D/F♯
D+/F♯
G
Bm7

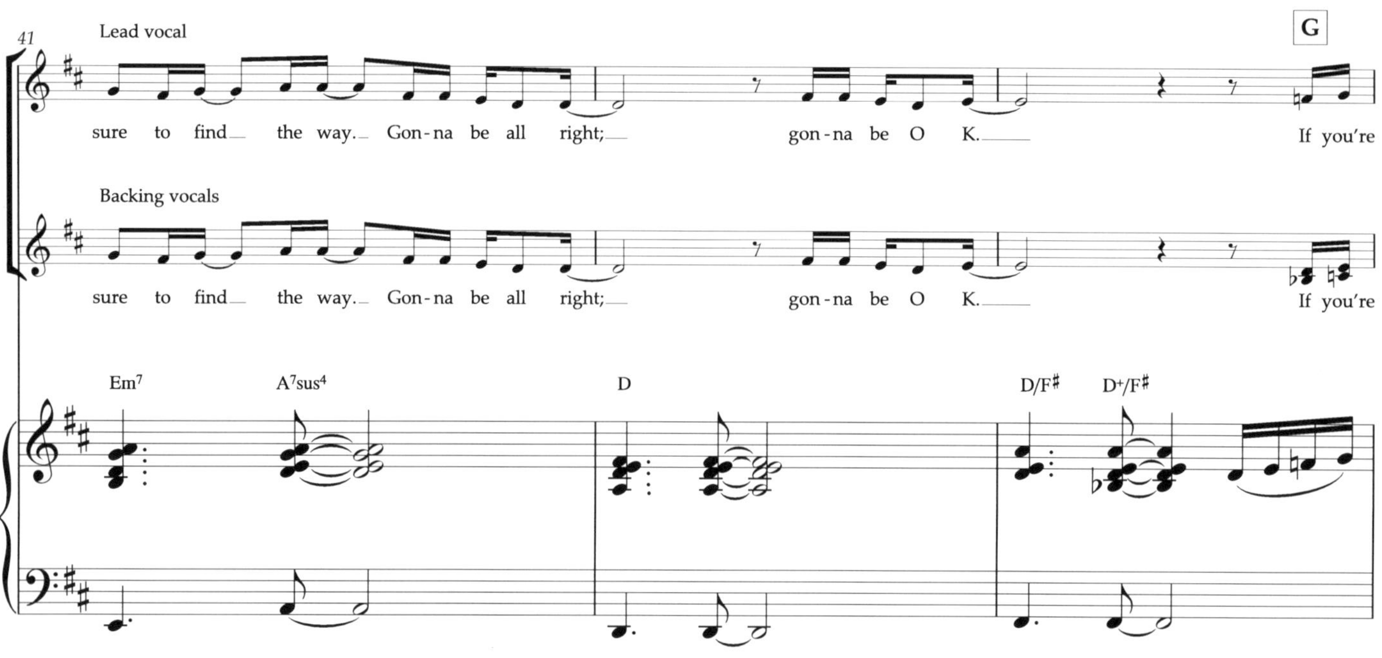
41
Lead vocal
G
sure to find the way. Gon-na be all right; gon-na be O K. If you're
Backing vocals
sure to find the way. Gon-na be all right; gon-na be O K. If you're
Em7
A7sus4
D
D/F♯
D+/F♯

44
reach-ing for the light, you're sure to find the way.
reach-ing for the light, you're sure to find the way.
B♭maj7
Am
Gm7
A7sus4
D
Bm/E
A7/F♯
Bm7/G
Bm7/A

RAPPED (*optional*):

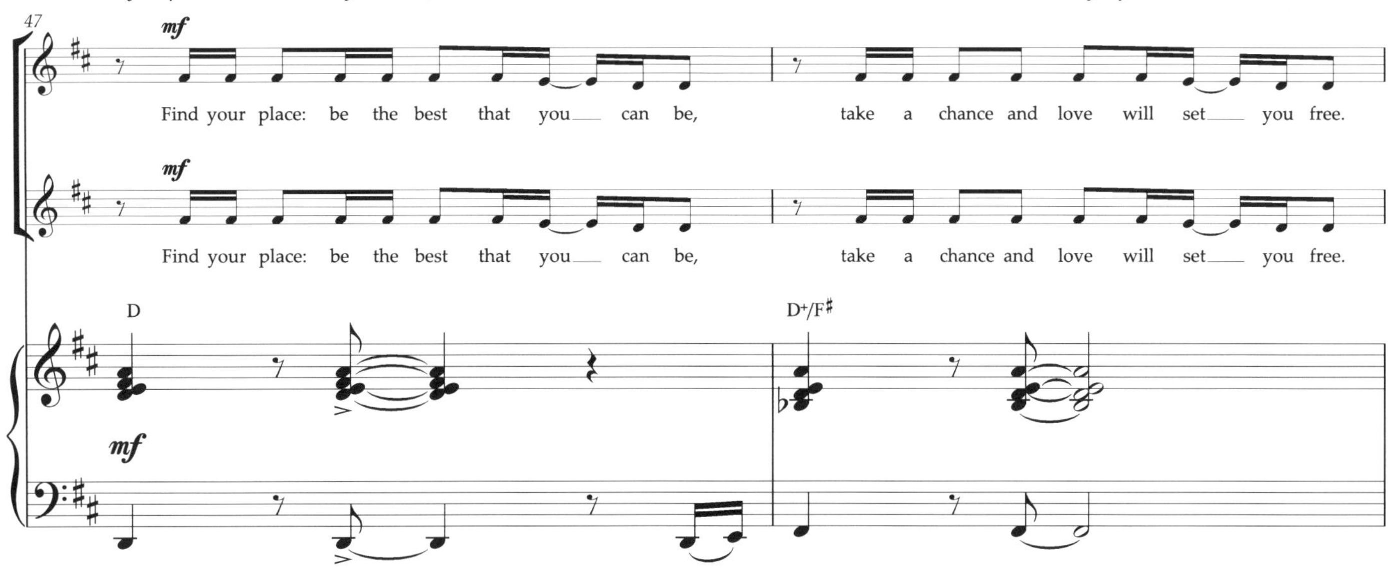

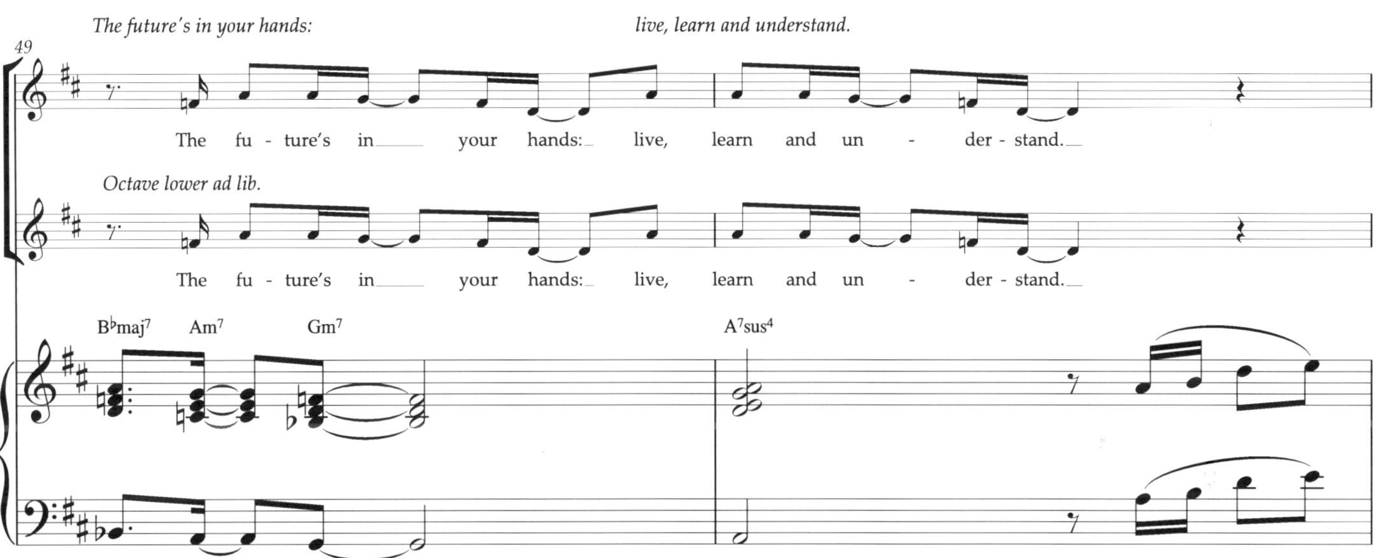

53
The future's in your hands: live, learn and understand.
The fu - ture's in your hands: live, learn and un - der - stand.
(Octave lower ad lib.)
The fu - ture's in your hands: live, learn and un - der - stand.
B♭maj7 Am7 Gm7
A7sus4
IMPROVISED SINGING (optional)
H
55
Gon - na be all right; gon - na be O K. If you're reach - ing for the light, you're
2nd time
Gon - na be all right; gon - na be O K. If you're reach - ing for the light, you're
2nd time
D
D+/F♯
B♭maj7 Am7 Gm9
RAPPED (in rhythm):
Take a chance: be the best that you can be,
58
sure to find the way. Gon - na be all right;
sure to find the way. Gon - na be all right;
Am7 G/A
D

find your place and love will set you free.
60
gon-na be O K. If you're reach - ing for the light, you're sure to find the way.
gon-na be O K. If you're reach - ing for the light, you're sure to find the way.
D+/F♯
B♭maj7
Am7
Gm9
Am7
G/A
63
Gon-na be all right; Gon-na be O K. If you're reach-ing for the light,
Gon-na be all right; Gon-na be O K. If you're reach-ing for the light,
D
D+/F♯
B♭maj7
Am7
Gm9
66
you're sure to find the way.
you're sure to find the way.
G/A
D

The Tyger

poem by
William Blake

music by
Steve Martland

13
In the fo - rests, in the fo - rests, in the fo - rests, in the fo - rests
In the fo - rests, in the fo - rests, in the fo - rests, in the fo - rests
17
of the night, of the night, of the night, of the night.
of the night, of the night, of the night, of the night.
A
21
f
Burn - ing bright, burn - ing bright, burn - ing bright, burn - ing bright, burn - ing bright, burn - ing bright, burn - ing bright, burn - ing bright,
f
What im - mor - tal hand or eye Could frame thy fear - ful sym - me - try?

B
25
burn - ing bright, burn - ing bright, burn - ing bright, burn - ing bright, burn - ing bright, burn - ing bright, burn - ing bright, burn - ing bright.
What im - mor - tal hand or eye Could frame thy fear - ful sym - me - try?
C
29
p
Ty - ger Ty - ger, Ty - ger Ty - ger, Ty - ger Ty - ger, Ty - ger Ty - ger,
p
Ty - ger Ty - ger, Ty - ger Ty - ger, Ty - ger Ty - ger, Ty - ger Ty - ger,
p
p
D
33
f
In what dis - tant deeps or skies Burnt the fire of thine eyes?
f
Burn - ing, burn - ing bright, burn - ing, burn - ing bright, burn - ing, burn - ing bright, burn - ing, burn - ing bright,
f
f
f

37
E
On what wings dare he a - spire? What the hand dare seize the fire?
burn-ing, burn-ing bright, burn-ing, burn-ing bright, burn-ing, burn-ng bright, burn-ing, burn-ing bright,
41
F
p
In the fo-rests, in the fo-rests, in the fo-rests, in the fo-rests.
p
In the fo-rests, in the fo-rests, in the fo-rests, in the fo-rests.
p
p
45
G
f
Ty-ger Ty-ger Ty-ger, Ty-ger Ty-ger Ty-ger, Ty-ger Ty-ger Ty-ger, Ty-ger Ty-ger Ty-ger,
f
And what shoul - der, and what art, Could twist the sin - ews of thy heart? And
mf
mf
mf

H
49
Ty-ger Ty-ger Ty-ger, Ty-ger Ty-ger Ty-ger, Ty-ger Ty-ger Ty-ger, Ty-ger Ty-ger Ty-ger,
when thy heart be - gan to beat, What dread hand? And what dread feet?
I
53
f
Ty-ger Ty-ger, Ty-ger Ty-ger, Ty-ger Ty-ger, Ty-ger Ty-ger,
p (echo)
In the fo-rests, in the fo-rests, in the fo-rests, in the fo-rests.
J
57
What the ham - mer? What the chain? In what fur - nace was thy brain? What the an - vil? What dread grasp?
Ty-ger Ty-ger Ty-ger, Ty-ger Ty-ger Ty-ger, Ty-ger Ty-ger Ty-ger, Ty-ger Ty-ger Ty-ger, Ty-ger
mf

60
K
Dare its dead - ly ter - rors clasp?
Ty-ger Ty-ger Ty-ger, Ty-ger Ty-ger Ty-ger, Ty-ger Ty-ger Ty-ger,
Ty - ger Ty-ger Ty-ger Ty-ger Ty-ger, What the ham - mer? What the chain? In what fur - nace was thy brain?
63
L
p
Ty-ger Ty-ger Ty-ger, Ty-ger Ty-ger Ty-ger, Ty-ger Ty-ger Ty-ger, Ty-ger Ty-ger,
f
What the an - vil? What dread grasp? Dare its dead - ly ter - rors clasp? In the fo-rests,
f
p
66
M
f
Ty - ger Ty - ger, Ty - ger Ty - ger, Ty - ger Ty - ger, When the
f
in the fo-rests, in the fo-rests, in the fo-rests. When the stars threw

70
stars threw down their spears And wa - tered hea - ven with their tears, When the stars threw
down their spears And wa - tered hea - ven with their tears, When the stars threw down their spears
74
down their spears And wa - tered hea - ven with their tears.
And wa - tered hea - ven with their tears.
3/2
f
78
N
f
Did he smile his work to see? Did he who made the Lamb make thee?
Ty-ger Ty-ger Ty-ger, Ty-ger Ty-ger Ty-ger, Ty-ger Ty-ger Ty-ger,

81
O
Did he smile his work to see? Did he who made the Lamb make thee? Ty - ger Ty - ger,
Ty-ger Ty-ger Ty-ger, Ty-ger Ty-ger Ty-ger, Ty-ger Ty-ger Ty-ger, Ty - ger Ty - ger, burn-ing bright
84
burn - ing bright In the fo - rests of the night, Ty - ger Ty - ger, burn - ing bright In the fo - rests
In the fo - rests of the night, Ty - ger Ty - ger, burn-ing bright In the fo - rests of the night.
87
P
of the night. What im - mor - tal hand or eye Dare frame thy fear -
What im - mor - tal hand or eye Dare frame thy fear - ful sym-me -

91
- ful sym - me - try? What im - mor - tal hand or eye Dare frame thy fear - ful sym - me - try?
- try? What im - mor - tal hand or eye Dare frame thy fear - ful sym - me - try?
Q
96
f
Ty - ger Ty - ger, Ty - ger Ty - ger, Ty - ger Ty - ger, Ty - ger Ty - ger,
f
In the fo - rests, in the fo - rests, in the fo - rests, in the fo - rests,
f
f
f
R
100
dim.
pp
Ty - ger Ty - ger, Ty - ger Ty - ger, In the fo - rests. Ty - ger Ty - ger.
dim.
pp
Ty - ger Ty - ger, Ty - ger Ty - ger, In the fo - rests. Ty - ger Ty - ger.
pp
dim.
pp
dim.
pp

Mo li hua

(Jasmine flower)

traditional Chinese
(Jiangsu province)

traditional Chinese melody
arranged by Cheng Yu

13
Hao yi duo mei li de mo li hua Fen fang mei li man zhi ya
come to my hand, lit - tle jas - mine flower. Ten - der shin - ing scent - ed star,
hua ya mo li hua; Mo li hua ya mo li hua; Mo li hua
flower, my jas - mine flower; jas - mine flower, my jas - mine flower; jas - mine flower,
17
You xiang you bai ren ren kua Rang wo lai jiang ni zhai xia
though I love you where you are I shall pluck you from a - bove;
mo li hua. Rang wo lai jiang ni zhai xia
jas - mine flower. I shall pluck you from a - bove;
21
Song gei bie ren jia Mo li hua, mo li hua.
give you to my love: jas - mine flower, jas - mine flower.
Song gei bie ren jia Mo li hua, mo li hua.
give you to my love: jas - mine flower, jas - mine flower.
f
26

31
Lively (𝅗𝅥 = 76)
C
f
Hao yi duo mei li de mo li hua
Come to my hand, lit-tle jas - mine flower,
Hao yi duo mei li de
Come to my hand, lit-tle
Lively (𝅗𝅥 = 76)
36
Fen fang mei li man zhi ya
ten - der shin - ing scent - ed star.
You xiang you bai ren ren
Though I love you from a -
mo li hua
jas - mine flower,
ten - der shin - ing scent - ed star.
40
D
kua.
- far:
Mo li hua,
jas - mine flower,
mo li hua
jas - mine flower.
Ya mo li hua ya
white jas - mine flower,
ya mo li hua ya
white jas - mine flower.

45
E
f
Yi ya yi ya yi er you ai ya ai zi you.
Hao yi duo mei li de mo li hua
Come to my hand, lit-tle jas-mine flower,
Yi ya yi ya yi er you ai ya ai zi you.
Hao yi duo mei li de
Come to my hand, lit-tle
50
Hao yi duo mei li de mo li hua
come to my hand, lit-tle jas-mine flower.
Fen fang mei li man zhi ya
Ten-der shin-ing scent-ed star,
You xiang you bai ren ren
though I love you from a-
mo li hua
jas-mine flower,
Hao yi duo mei li de mo li hua
come to my hand, lit-tle jas-mine flower.
Fen fang mei li man zhi ya
Ten-der shin-ing scent-ed star,
55
kua ya.
-far.
You xiang you bai ren ren kua ya kua ya mo li hua.
Though I love you from a-far, my sweet jas-mine flower.
You xiang you bai ren ren kua ya.
though I love you from a-far.
You xiang you bai ren ren kua ya mo li hua.
Though I love you from a-far; sweet jas-mine flower.
mf

* the melody is shared between the two voices, as reflected in the dynamics.

76
mp
mf
Rang wo lai jiang ni zhai xia Song gei bie ren jia Mo li
I shall pluck you from a - bove; give you to my love: jas - mine
mf
mp
Rang wo lai jiang ni zhai xia Song gei bie ren jia Mo li
I shall pluck you from a - bove; give you to my love: jas - mine
80
mp
hua, mo li hua. Rang wo lai jiang ni zhai xia
flower, jas - mine flower. I shall pluck you from a - bove;
mf
hua, mo li hua. Rang wo lai jiang ni zhai xia
flower, jas - mine flower. I shall pluck you from a - bove;
84
mf
rall.
Song gei bie ren jia mo li hua.
give you to my love: jas - mine flower.
mp
Song gei bie ren jia mo li hua.
give you to my love: jas - mine flower.
rall.

Harmony

lyrics by
Eugene & Yami Skeef

music by
Eugene Skeef

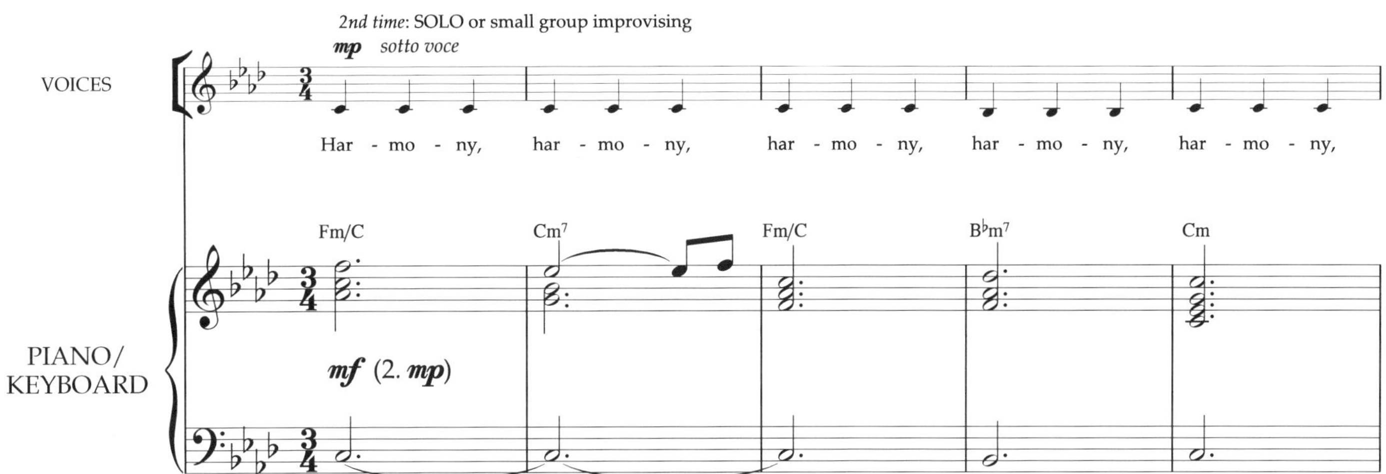

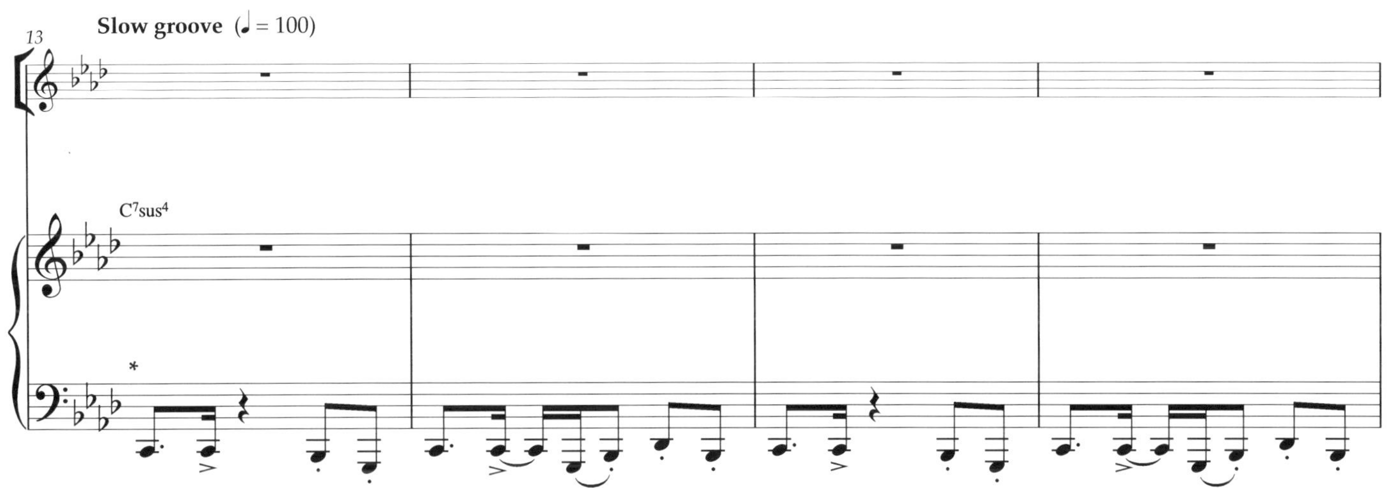

* add bass guitar if possible

*Zulu: 'We are in harmony'

Slow groove (♩ = 100)
B
optional interlude (not in recording)
to continue
VOICES
ALL
We are
BASS GUITAR (or PIANO L. H.)
to continue
CABASSA, SHAKER
to continue
BONGOS, CONGAS
BASS DRUM
one fa - mi - ly, spawned from the
repeat rhythm to E
repeat rhythm to E
repeat rhythm to E
same wa - ters; each but a par - ti - cle
in the vast o - cean of hu - ma - ni - ty.
Our hearts beat in time to the call of the

50
first sun - - rise, wit - nessed on the
first sun - - rise, wit - nessed on the
first sun - - rise, wit - nessed on the
55
morn - - ing of our mo - ther's song ...
59
We are one fa - mi - ly,
64
spawned from the same wa - ters;
C
69
each but a par - ti - cle in the
73
vast o - cean of hu - ma - ni - ty. Our

77
hearts beat in time to the call of the
81
first sun - - - rise,
first sun - - - rise,
first sun - - - rise,
D
(ALL)
85
wit-nessed on the morn - ing of our mo-ther's song ...
Slow groove (♩ = 100)
E
90
Fm9
Cm7(add4)
f
8
HI-HAT or TAMBOURINE
HANDCLAPS or SNARE
BASS DRUM

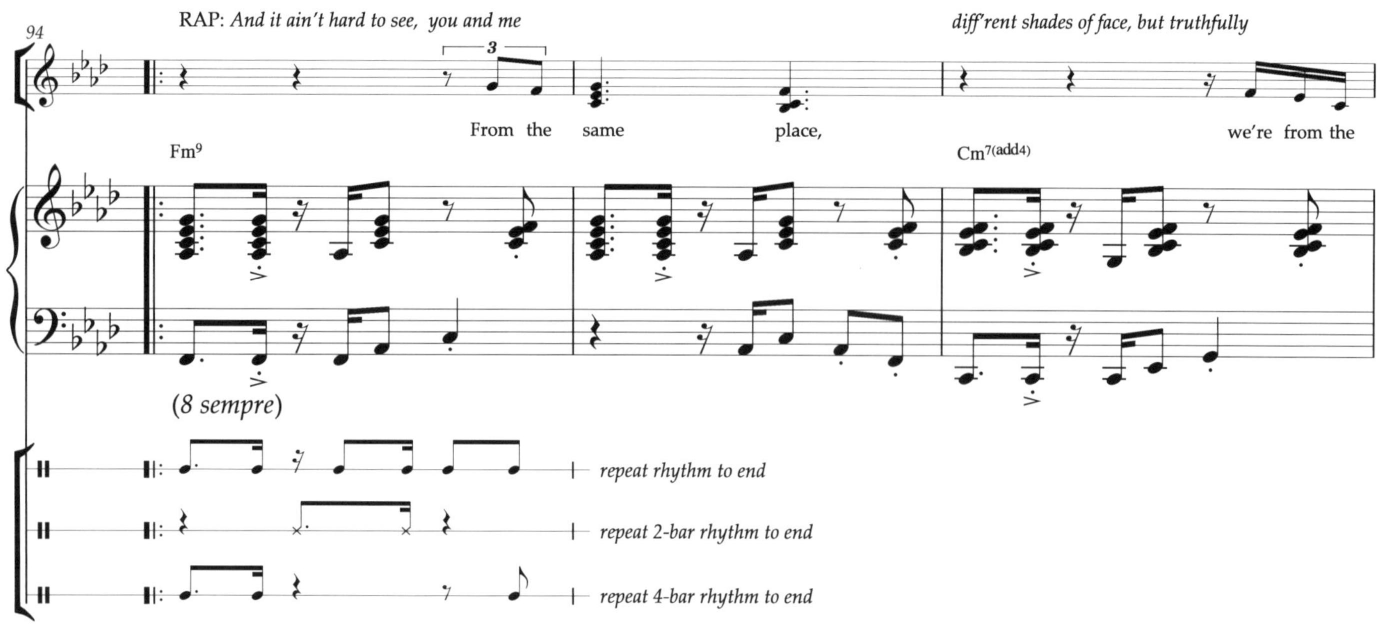

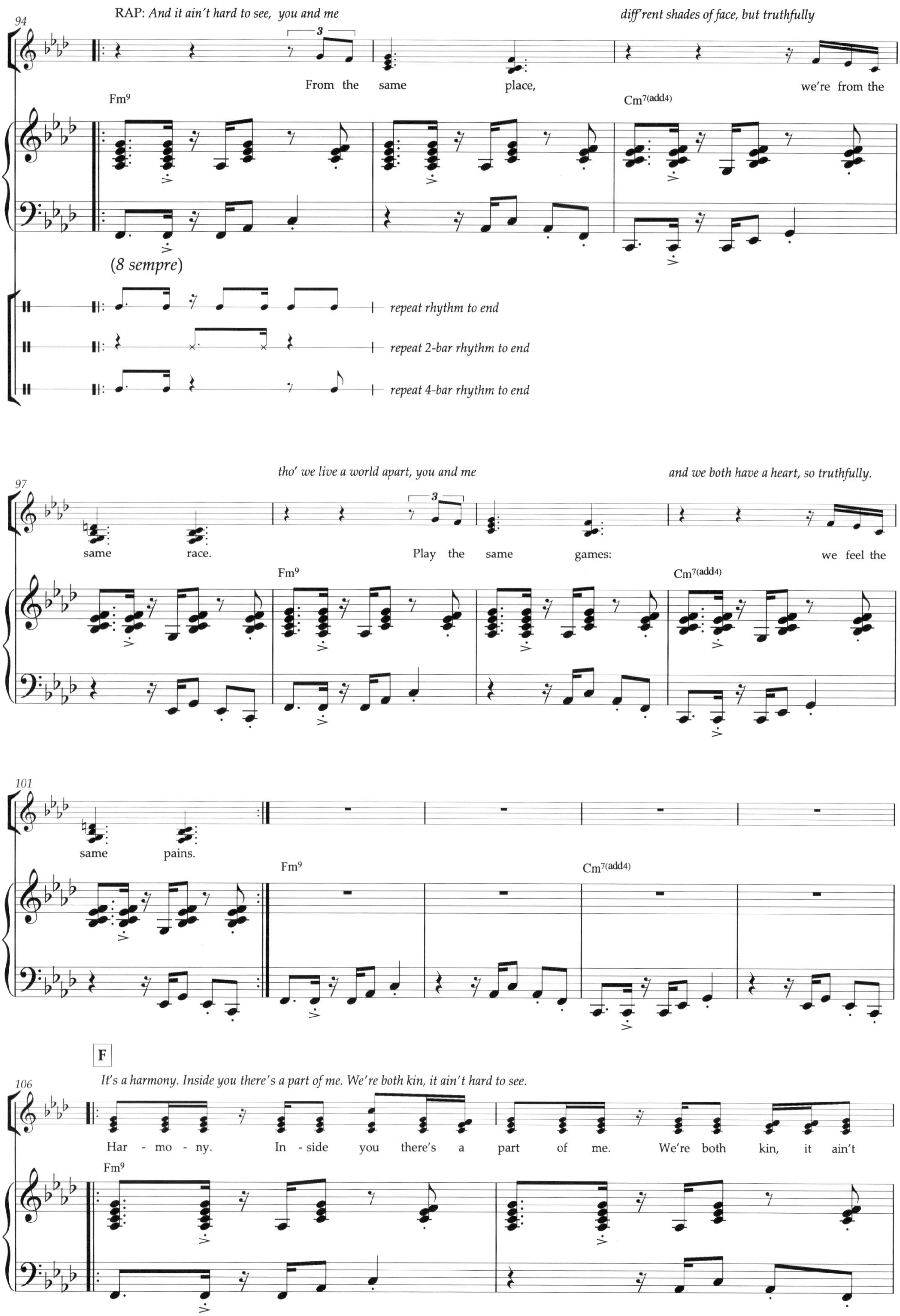

97

tho' we live a world apart, you and me

and we both have a heart, so truthfully.

3

same race. Play the same games: we feel the

Fm9

Cm7(add4)

101

same pains.

Fm9

Cm7(add4)

108
It's like the rain and the moon and the stars and the sea.
1., 2., 3.
repeat 4 times
4.
hard to see. It's like the rain and the moon and the stars and the sea. It's a moon and the stars and the sea.
Cm7(add4)
G
111
SOLO or small group
Oo
ALL
Har - mo - ny. In - side you there's a part of me. We're both kin, it ain't hard to see. It's like the rain and the
Fm9
Cm7(add4)
114
oo
moon and the stars and the sea. It's a har - mo - ny. In - side you there's a part of me. We're both kin, it ain't
Fm9
117
repeat and fade
hard to see. It's like the rain and the moon and the stars and the sea. It's a
Cm7(add4)

No wars will stop us singing

lyrics by
Don Black

music by
Debbie Wiseman

22
wars will stop us sing-ing; our voic - es will stay
B♭ E♭/F B♭ E♭/F B♭ E♭/F
mf
28
strong. E - ven through the dark - est night
B♭ E♭/A Gm F E♭ B♭/D Cm Cm/B♭
C
stronger
34
we will sing our song. No fear will stop us
A♭ F B♭ E♭/F
40
dream - ing; our dreams will light the sky.
B♭ E♭/F B♭ E♭/F B♭ E♭/A

D
46
Lead vocal
mf
E - ven when all hope is gone our dreams will not
Backing vocal
mf
E - ven when all hope is gone our dreams will not
Gm F E♭ B♭/D Cm Cm/B♭ A♭
52
E
Bold, with intensity
die. We are the fu - ture; we are to - mor - row;
die. We are the fu - ture; we are to-
Bold, with intensity
F Gm F/A E♭/B♭ F/A
58
cresc. poco a poco
we are the peace that you all crave. If our lives are ta - ken we'll
- mor - row; the peace that you all crave. We'll
Gm E♭ F E♭/F Gm F/A
64
F
f strong
sing from be - yond the grave. No
cresc. poco a poco
f strong
sing from be - yond the grave. No
E♭ F Gm7/C F F7 E♭/F

70
wars will stop us sing - ing; our voic - es will stay
B♭ E♭/F B♭ E♭/F B♭ E♭/F
76
strong. E - ven through the dark - est night
B♭ E♭/A Gm F E♭ B♭/D Cm Cm/B♭
G
with power
82
we will sing our song. We will sing, we will
A♭ A♭/G F A♭ E♭ Fm7
89
ff
sing, we must sing our song.
E♭ D♭ G♭ Fsus4 F B♭
96
rit.
E♭/F B♭ E♭/F B♭ E♭/F B♭

Join our campaign for singing @

WWW.SINGBOOK.ORG.UK

Youth Music is running a campaign to promote and support singing in all its forms. We need your help with this. Please log on to www.singbook.org.uk and join our campaign. The Singbook website is a complementary on-line resource for use by music leaders, teachers and the young singers themselves. Time-saving and easy to use, www.singbook.org.uk :

- Provides well-researched support materials and imaginative teaching tools for all Singbook users.
- Develops good practice: each song web page provides all the warm ups especially devised for that particular song as printable downloads – with some extra warm ups only available on-line – to help your singers master some of its more challenging aspects in an enjoyable way.
- Helps Singbook users to understand and interpret each song in its wider context, with information and specific web links to help music leaders explore the social, historical and creative themes for each song.
- Encourages your group to become songwriters: discover simple and effective ways to develop lyrics, melodies and accompaniments.
- Presents audio material on-line: extracts of the songs are given to help you to decide which song to try next.
- Contains downloadable MP3 Utility Mixes of some of the songs for DJ-ing and sampling, to create your own unique versions of the songs.
- Gives other repertoire ideas: 'More songs like this!' suggests other music by the same composer, in the same genre or about the same topic, helping you to expand your repertoire and devise successful programmes. There's also the option for you to suggest your own similar song or exercise.
- Provides simple instrumental parts as downloads for selected songs.
- Allows you to print out all downloadable material: although you can photocopy from the book, you might find it more effective to hand out colour lyric sheets, downloaded from the site.

SO SHARE YOUR IDEAS AND EXPERIENCES ONLINE AND JOIN THE YOUTH MUSIC CAMPAIGN FOR SINGING!